Praise for

BET ON YOU!
BUILD ON SUCCESSFUL STRATEGIES
B.O.S.S.

"Tonya Kilpatrick is the motivators' motivator. BET ON YOU! was created for the motivator. Reading this book will help you to reignite your passions encourage you to 'Unpack Your Dreams.' This book will help you do a self-evaluation. After reading it you will be equipped to be the leader you were created to be. Bet on You is designed to motivate men and women to achieve their highest level of success in every area of their life. Your life will be completely transformed, and you will become an influencer because of it."
-**Coach Maston Knowles**, Life Coach, Leadership Developer, Customer Service Consultant, *IMotivate, LLC*

"Tonya Kilpatrick will certainly 'ignite your dynamite' as she shares her story of trauma as a result of the loss of her mother, dropping out of high school, and becoming a mother—all in her teen years. She gracefully walks you through her life's journey with eye-opening and profound nuggets of wisdom that will prompt one to reflect as well as take action. This amazing story of perseverance will encourage other women to persevere and take risks to help them know that SELF is the one to BET on!"

-**Lisa Ann Johnson, M.A.**, The Crownselor™

"This book should be in demand! In my opinion, it is the manual of instruction for winning in life. The strategies in this book are spot on. Anyone that wants to WIN, come aboard. Thanks Tonya."

-**Nomad Londan**, Financial Analyst

"Bet on You! Build on Successful Strategies ~ BOSS is a book about finding your purpose and acting on it. This book takes you on a journey of a resilient life. A journey of obstacles overcome by strategically thinking and taking action. She teaches you about successful strategies used by others to achieve their successes. Tonya then takes those strategies to teach you to how to operationalize your dreams. You come away feeling like you know her, and you leave with a plan."

-**John Barfield**, MBA

"Great Read. Very insightful. This book is amazing, Bet on You! BOSS lays out a plan that will help you put your career and life goals in perspective. A game-changer for career progression."

-Twanna Kilpatrick, CEO
T's Sweet and Savory Kitchen

"Bet on You is the culmination of an astounding journey that reveals valuable strategies to enable you to live the life you desire to live. It has given me incredible insight into what it truly means to play the winning hand. Tonya Kilpatrick has provided clear, effective methodology on how to win and win big; in spite of the hand that life deals you."

-Alexandra E. Carter, Entrepreneur and Motivational Speaker

"BET ON YOU! BUILD ON SUCCESSFUL STRATEGIES is a blueprint to help you succeed in any business. The 'Ace High' model is a masterful game-changer to achieve a winning outcome in business and life."

-Joe Peleg, Founder, CEO, Innovator
Friends Beverage Group, LLC, (Fun Wine)

Bet on You!

Build On Successful Strategies
B.O.S.S.

Bet on You!

Build On Successful Strategies
B.O.S.S.

TONYA KILPATRICK, MBA
WITH FOREWORD BY LES BROWN

SBPC

SIMMS BOOKS PUBLISHING CORPORATION

Publishers Since 2012

Published By Simms Books Publishing

Jonesboro, GA

Foreword by Les Brown

Copyright ©Tonya Kilpatrick, MBA, 2021

All rights reserved. No part of this book may be reproduced, scanned, or distributed in any print or electronic form without permission. Please do not participate in or encourage piracy of copyrighted materials in violation of the author's rights. Purchase only authorized editions.

Library of Congress Cataloging in Publication Data

2020925500

Tonya Kilpatrick, MBA

Bet On You!

BUILD ON SUCCESSFUL STRATEGIES

B.O.S.S.

ISBN: 978-0-578-54553-0

Printed in the United States of America

Cover photo: Nick "Brandprenuer" Nelson

Cover design: Korean Kay

DEDICATION

To my late mother, Mae Helen, who inspired me to believe in myself and to always *Bet on Me*.

I gladly dedicate this book to achieving goals, dreams, and successes by Building on Successful Strategies to advance your mental, spiritual, and physical capabilities—one hundred percent!

"Ability is what you're capable of doing. Motivation determines what you do. Attitude determines how well you do it."

~ LOU HOLTZ

Table of Contents

Acknowledgement	i
Foreword by Les Brown	v
Introduction	vii

Chapter 1
BE A BOSS — 1

Chapter 2
DEFINE YOURSELF — 5

Chapter 3
INVEST IN YOURSELF:
YOU ARE WORTH IT — 9

Chapter 4
SUCCESS IS INTENTIONAL — 13

Chapter 5
BUILD YOUR CONFIDENCE — 19

Chapter 6
WHEN THE HORSE DIES, DISMOUNT — 25

Chapter 7
START THINKING ABOUT
RESULTS: BE A STAR — 29

Chapter 8
SET BOUNDARIES:
LOVE YOURSELF — 35

Chapter 9 KNOW YOUR VALUE: DO NOT EXPECT OTHERS TO CALCULATE IT FOR YOU ... 41

Chapter 10 YOUR FRIENDS BECOME YOU (AND VICE VERSA) ... 49

Chapter 11 BE EXTRAORDINARY: EXCELLENCE IS THE NORM, NOT THE EXCEPTION ... 55

Chapter 12 ELEVATE YOUR CHARACTER ... 59

Chapter 13 SET MEASURABLE GOALS ... 63

Chapter 14 BET ON YOU! ... 67

CONCLUSION ... 73

ACKNOWLEDGEMENTS

Where do I begin? There are so many to thank. During the time I spent developing the ideas for *Bet on You! Build on Success Strategies ~ BOSS*, I benefitted from the inspiration and support of mentors, coaches, family, friends, associates, colleagues, and countless others.

I am so grateful for the opportunity to share my testimony and do the work that I was created for – inspiring and empowering others to achieve success and Greatness. I want to acknowledge those who have contributed to getting this book into your hands:

To my forever friend, Kenneth, thank you for believing in me when I didn't believe in myself and for encouraging me to write this book. You know the story up close and personal – the good, the bad, and the ugly.

To the dedicated team at Simms Books Publishing Corporation, thank you for believing in me and my story, and for encouraging me and crystalizing the vision – especially James Simms and Mary Hoekstra.

To my children Kenneth II, Brittany "Korean Kay" and Dominique, thank you so much for your support, editorial touches, critical insight, encouragement, and belief in me. Through the hurdles, obstacles, and frustrations, you kept me motivated and focused to press forward. I love you with all my heart. I am blessed to be your mother and have your never-ending love and support.

To my grandchildren, Lexxington, Kenneth III, Sanai, Lia, and Honesty, thank you for your patience and for loving me to the sun and back. You all are my special heartbeat. I am honored to be your "Gi-Gi."

To my sisters Alexandra Carter and Twanna Kilpatrick, thank you for being a sounding board and continuous source of inspiration, encouragement, and support.

To Dr. Dennis Kimbro, thank you for your vision, coaching, guidance, and insightfulness that inspired me out of my comfort zone and provoked me towards achieving my destiny, unapologetically and without compromise.

To Les Brown, thank you for believing in me, coaching me, and stretching me to maximize my Greatness and raise my level of vision. During this journey, you taught me to never make a point without telling a story and never tell a story without making a point.

To the Most High, for gifting me with the passion to inspire, empower and elevate others to live the life they were created to live on purpose. Because of YOU, I am. Thank You for the opportunity to solve a problem and make an impact.

Foreword

by Les Brown

You have something special; you've got GREATNESS in YOU! If you have followed my career or heard me speak, then you know that I believe that each of us has been blessed with special and unique gifts that we are destined to share with the Universe.

We are made on purpose and with a purpose, but unfortunately-- many of us go to our graves without ever truly tapping into what that purpose really is. We settle and then we stop. We are told that we aren't good enough, or even worse, we believe that "just good enough" is enough for our lives. We convince ourselves that as long as we have a roof over our head and a job to pay our bills, then we're doing just fine.

What if I told you that doing just fine...is a myth? It truly serves you no good to be just fine when you were made to **dominate and shine.**

When I was growing up, we were told that you shouldn't gamble and for quite a while, it was illegal. Well, today is a new day, and even though I don't gamble, I'm willing to bet that you haven't even scratched the surface of the amazing opportunities, experiences, wealth, and of course - greatness that life has in store for you.

Will you take me up on that wager?

In **Bet on You,** Tonya Kilpatrick shares her powerful story of going from a GED to a graduate degree, and from struggle to success, and how you can do the same.

If you are ready to turn the corner to walk into your destiny, you're in the right place. I'm here to tell you that there is so much more waiting for you than you can ever imagine.

I want to encourage you to **Bet on You.** Start today by reading this book! Tonya shares strategies and tools for your personal success that will prepare you to uncover and overcome the mental and emotional barriers that stand between where you are now, and the life that you were born to live!

I believe that Tonya Kilpatrick has the gifts of motivation, inspiration, and wisdom. She knows, like I do, that when you **Bet on You,** you can't lose!

That's my story and I'm sticking to it.

Yours in GREATNESS,

Les Brown

Speaker, Author, Trainer

INTRODUCTION

"The diameter of a man's knowledge determines the circumference of his movements."

~ JAMES COLBERT

Don't despise the process on your journey. Success is the gradual process of manifesting your goals. This book is a practical, inspirational, empowering, and pragmatic approach to encourage you to achieve your goals and dreams while succeeding in the game of life without compromise.

This book will serve as a blueprint to discover your truth, highlight how amazing you are, and reveal that you were created with everything you need to succeed.

You have so much to offer to the world, and most importantly, *yourself!* The words in this book tell you of my personal trials and how my strength was revealed. I liken it to the process of making a diamond; through immense heat and pressure a lump of coal becomes refined, brilliant, strong, with perfect clarity. I am more than a survivor; and flourished because of the principles I am sharing with you in this book.

Without a test there is no testimony. If you implement the things I suggest, you will play the game of life by your own rules and be empowered to live the BOSS life!

1

BE A BOSS

"Remind yourself every day that you're in it to win it. You are your most valuable asset. Do what you need to do to make it happen! You have GREATNESS within you!"

~ LES BROWN

BET ON YOU!

If you refuse to choose, you lose. You have the absolute power to be anyone you want to be. There is nothing you cannot do. It is up to you. The journey is just beginning. Ignite your dynamite!

You are the CEO of your life. You are the boss and master of your destiny. Be creative with the greatness that came before you. Use lessons learned and successful strategies to reinvent, realign and adapt. You will either evolve or become extinct.

You must know how to execute your plan with practices and behaviors that produce favorable results. Along with the practices, you must have a plan of action and strategies. Both your practices and your strategies must align to position you for success.

To achieve your goals, you must be willing to do whatever is necessary to obtain your desired results. *The best way out is always through!* (Robert Frost). Successful people know how to innovate and be resourceful. You are greater than your mistakes and your past. Take it from me, someone who has learned to make better decisions to neutralize past mistakes.

There is evidence as to why someone or something succeeds. A keen eye and the power of observation will provide all the tools you need to accomplish your goals. Pay attention. Evaluate what works and why. Carefully study the methods of the best in uniqueness, personality, and style. If something works, build on it and make it great!

Once a boss figures out the system of success, they re-engineer and fine-tune it. They can create, replicate, and follow a winning formula.

> There are three types of people:
> 1. Those who lead the majority;
> 2. Those who follow the majority; and
> 3. Those who are a majority of one.

Bosses are independent thinkers who do not outsource their thinking. They do not follow the masses; instead, they lead.

They are agents of change who are proactive problem solvers, focused, and decisive. They create what they desire. Bosses possess the power of persuasion and influence. They are strategic and take risks to get results.

Activate your mojo—that undefinable energy that creates upon itself. When you have it, you know it. When you possess it, it is apparent to the world.

BET ON YOU!

Bosses push others to achieve greatness. When they speak, people will listen. They possess the "it factor" that results in instant attraction and powerful credibility.

As I grew in knowledge and stature and progressed through my career, I caught the attention of some incredible coaches who took me under their wings and became my mentors.

One of my mentors challenged me to actualize my potential. She demonstrated how to lead and practiced the art of negotiation to facilitate a win-win. I began to model my behavior, communication, conduct, and style of dress after her. She was a significant influence on my professional development process.

Be a consistent franchise player who wins wherever you go. Never settle for the bare minimum. You must reach a point where you want to win and achieve greatness as vital as the need to breathe. Be bold and daring—the greater the risk, the greater the reward. You must make sacrifices to obtain what you want.

Everything costs. Be brutally honest. Ask yourself tough questions like, "Am I a BOSS?" "Do I have it?" "Am I who I want to be?" "Am I willing to do what it takes to have what I desire?"

BE A BOSS

Put together a calculated plan and start visualizing the new you. Excellence is the norm, not the exception. Strive for excellence and accept nothing less. Rise to the top and become recognized as a brand of excellence. The things you desire, want, and yearn for all involve a process.

"Whosoever desires constant success must change his conduct with the times."

~ Niccolò Machiavelli

2

DEFINE YOURSELF

"In a world full of game players, the only way to set yourself apart is to be a game-changer."
~ Matshona Dhliwayo

BET ON YOU!

Don't allow circumstances to define your outcome. Situations occur, but your reaction is the defining variable.

Anybody can play a good hand and win. It takes tenacity, passion, drive, and determination to play a bad hand and win. I did not start with a good hand. I was not trumped tight, and I did not have any aces in my deck.

I was a young, 16-year-old teenage mother and a high school dropout, living on food stamps, Section 8 housing, and government assistance to survive. On top of that, my 33-year-old mother passed away, leaving behind four young children when my infant son was only three months old. I was the oldest of my siblings. My sister was 11 years old, and my brothers were 9 and 7 years old. A major loss for all of us.

Despite those setbacks, I became empowered to get an education and achieve levels of seemingly unattainable success. I went from having a GED to earning an MBA. How did I accomplish this? By maintaining a mindset of unstoppable tenacity and achievement despite the odds. You can, too.

My mother lost her leg when she was 22 years old. As a child, I watched her navigate life effectively, on crutches, with one leg as if she had two. She even gave birth to my three younger siblings. Her disability was never an excuse; it was a reason to succeed despite her physical limitations. She did everything a person with two legs could do.

My biological father was convicted for a murder he did not commit when he was 17 years old. He was sentenced to life in prison without parole. I was just an infant. Eventually, his conviction was overturned. My mother got married during the time of his incarceration and my new father accepted me as his own. I never developed a father-daughter relationship with my biological father.

When I say, "Do not allow circumstances to define your outcome," I am speaking from experience. My mother taught me that principle. She was a prime example of that and passed it on to my siblings and me. As a result, depending on others was not something I wanted. I desired more.

Today's ceiling is tomorrow's floor. When my son was still an infant, I went to work at a local fast-food restaurant to make enough money to take care of him. I was also breastfeeding him at that time.

While working at the restaurant, the manager demanded that I mop the entire outside of the restaurant. I took the mop, stared at it, and analyzed the situation. With the pain and rush of breast milk streaming down my uniform and tears in my eyes at 16 years old, I immediately decided how to respond...

I quit. I did it that day and felt empowered!

The choice I made that day was one of the best decisions of my life. It fueled my ambition, energy, and desire to transform. Although I was on my own with a small child and had no money, I trusted myself enough to know that if something had to be, it was up to me.

Overcoming all those obstacles felt impossible at first. Instead, I changed "impossible" to "I am possible." I had to protect my dream and focus on my will to succeed.

The trajectory of my life changed. Navigating the journey was a process with many obstacles and stepping stones. That experience helped me to persevere, despite the odds and endure, regardless of my circumstances.

I did not allow what I faced to define my outcome. I am a survivor who defied statistics and shattered the status quo. Success is a choice.

You must understand how to use your mind's wisdom and the power of your will to program your behavior to reach your desired outcome. Changing your decisions will change your behavior. Your life is not a sequence of random chances, it is a series of intentional choices. You define yourself! You have the sole and absolute power to become anyone you want to be.

"Circumstances do not make the man, they reveal him."

~ JAMES ALLEN

3

**INVEST IN
YOURSELF**
YOU ARE WORTH IT

"Don't sit down and wait for the opportunities to come, get up and make them."
~ Madam C.J. Walker

BET ON YOU!

*E*ducation is an equalizer, and knowledge is the new currency. Admit what you do not know, then learn it.

Never rest on your trophies. Do the work to achieve and accomplish more than you did before. This principle guides a continuous improvement mindset. You are only as great as your last success.

We invest money in our family, children, friends, and even habits but rarely invest in ourselves. My passion for excellence and a willingness to do the work keeps me motivated, even when I feel like giving up. I am continuously improving myself, no matter how far I have come. I learned the beauty of this firsthand when I dropped out of high school to have a baby at 16. I wanted more. The first step was to get a high school diploma and find a decent job that rewarded my worth and value. I studied very hard to earn my GED. When I received it in the mail, I achieved one of the highest scores in its history. It was such an exciting moment.

I landed a job as a secretary and became self-sufficient. I got off food stamps, Section 8 housing, and government assistance. I even purchased my first home when I was 23 years old. While working, I started observing and learning from different managers along the way.

I was like a sponge with a continuous thirst for all kinds

information. My managers recognized the potential in me that I did not see. I was in awe of them. As I grew, my thirst continued. I wanted more. Several years later, I was ready to try my hand at college. Yes, me.... The high school dropout with only a GED. I needed a degree to expand my opportunities and increase my earning potential in the job market.

While pregnant with my third child, I applied to Florida A&M University (FAMU). Coincidentally, this is the same University where I was born when they had a hospital on the campus --FAMU Hospital.

Also, my children attended its K-12 Developmental Research School (FAMU-DRS). As a first-generation college student, I was nervous. No one in my family had a college education. I would be establishing a new legacy.

The University responded to my application and requested that I write an essay about why I wanted a college education. I wondered, *How do I begin to articulate a compelling enough reason to be accepted into this legacy institution of higher learning?*

I wrote an essay detailing all the reasons I wanted a college education and how I would use the knowledge gained to help others succeed. At that time, I did not realize that I was writing the blueprint for my life.

I anxiously waited for my acceptance letter. When the acceptance letter arrived in the mail, I was shocked and excited at the same time!

I was proud to be accepted among some of the best students in the nation who, on average, attained a 1200 score on the Scholastic Assessment Test (SAT). On enrollment day, I proudly stepped onto that campus six months pregnant and ready to tackle the next phase of my life.

While in college, I worked a full-time job. I incurred a significant amount of debt to invest in my education and help support my household as a wife and mother.

The grooming process that followed enhanced my presence and catapulted my confidence, which shaped who I am today. The very first Dean of the School of Business and Industry (SBI), an astute businesswoman, renowned motivator, and prominent on many corporate boards, taught me what was necessary to achieve corporate success. I studied her, researched her, and watched her as she shattered traditional limitations. She instilled in me the foundation of what I am using today as a business executive. She embodied how to dress, how to speak, how to interact with others, and how to be a leader.

INVEST IN YOURSELF

During my junior year in college, my 8-year-old daughter was offered an exclusive modeling contract in Manhattan, New York. I decided to adjust my plan. It sounds crazy, but I welcomed the possibility of recreating myself.

I dropped out of college and invested in her chance at a modeling career. We relocated to New York. At the time, I thought I could finish college anywhere, even with three kids, no support, and nowhere to live. It was wishful thinking.

No matter what happens, do not predicate your worth or value based on the opinions of others. You are not a product of the opinionated masses who evaluate you. You are great because you are you.

While making moves to achieve whatever you desire, maintain your edge. Drain every drop of your talent and influence the world with it. Stand in your core values and excellence! Be great and make an impact wherever you go.

"People with goals succeed because they know where they're going."

~ EARL NIGHTINGALE

SUCCESS IS INTENTIONAL

"I attribute my success to this:— I never gave or took an excuse"

~ Florence Nightingale

BET ON YOU!

New York City. The largest city in the United States. I had never been to a city that size in my life. I was in over my head. The odds were stacked against me and felt insurmountable.

I had no job, no car, no friends, and no source of income. I was a college dropout in the most daunting metropolis in America! All I had was my suitcase, a few clothes, and a big reality check! Hello, reality.

I had a great aunt named Helen, my mother's namesake, who lived there, so I gave it a shot! I had hope that something greater was coming and was inspired.

Lights... Camera... Action! Your life is your performance. There are no dress rehearsals, and you only get one chance to perform your grand recital—you might even miss a note or two.

Sometimes, you must take a step backward to move forward. My children and I slept on my aunt's living room couch. She must have thought I was crazy to take on the Big Apple, the Empire State, and "the city that never sleeps." She was probably right! Despite that, she said to me, "If you can make it here, you can make it anywhere." That challenge continued to resonate within.

In between taking my daughter to her auditions as a child

model, I worked temp assignments during the day through a staffing agency. I was assigned to help law firms, typing depositions at night. Each day, I waited for the phone to ring for my next temporary job assignment while searching for stable employment and housing for my family.

My gamble finally paid off. One day, I took the train downtown and got off at Times Square. I walked to the corner of 64th Street and Broadway. I looked up and saw a tall building with five big letters— ASCAP—in red. At that moment, I knew I had found stable employment. I went inside the building, took the elevator up along with some celebrities, and I acted as if I was one too.

I walked into the Human Resources Department with a strong persona. I confidently requested a job. They said, "We may have something for you," and hired me that day.

Just like that, I had a brand-new start! I was with the in-crowd, and I was in style.

At the time, I was unaware that ASCAP (American Society of Composers, Artists and Publishers) was an organization of 700,000 songwriters, composers, and music publishers. I accepted a position working in the marketing department with a generous salary as a personal assistant to the senior vice president of marketing. He later became one of my mentors.

BET ON YOU!

While I was looking for a place to stay, I saw some beautiful brownstones. One stood out, and I knew that brownstone would be my new home. I learned that it was called "Striver's Row," where African Americans striving to achieve greatness resided during the Harlem Renaissance. I researched to find who the landlord was, spoke with him to express my interest, and we moved into our new place. My Great Aunt Helen was very proud! She bragged to her friends, "Tonya came up here and moved on Striver's Row!"

The first thing I did was enroll my children in private school. Then, I went shopping. I bought new clothes, new furniture, and a brand-new car straight off the showroom floor to cruise down 125th Street and through the city.

New York was one of the most incredible experiences of my life. I was on a winning streak and started reaping my rewards. The experience was a turning point for me because I had never taken such a huge risk. It solidified my character, my attitude, and my ability to deal with any situation in life.

Since I made it there, I knew I could make it anywhere. It gave me the belief that I could accomplish anything. It powerfully shattered my comfort zone. I had bet on myself and succeeded!

Why is it that the same set of circumstances can produce

different results for different people? It has more to do with your mindset and core beliefs in your gifts, talents, abilities, determination, tenacity, and perseverance.

What you want is already on the inside of you. You must own your thoughts and opinions. That is the key to tapping into your inherent greatness.

Ignite your dynamite! Reprogram any negative self-talk. See what you believe rather than believing what you see.

Build your confidence and strengthen your character. Make yourself a powerful asset by becoming accomplished, developing integrity, and earning credibility.

Avoid addictive behaviors and toxic individuals.

The things you are looking for are looking for you. Are you willing to do what it takes to have what you want? Life is not a sequence of chances. It is a series of choices. You can have whatever you like. Seize it!

When you find that everything around you is falling apart, sometimes you must make a bold move away from the familiar. Be daring. I did it!

In New York I experienced the most powerful journey of My life in one of America's toughest cities. It was a great move. Looking back on it now, I cannot believe I dared to do it.

BET ON YOU!

It takes determination to leave what is safe and comfortable.

When you read or hear stories about successful people, they often reached a point where they were either forced to leave their comfort zones or became sick and tired of the status quo. It gave them the impetus to call on their courage and move!

I live by the philosophy that the best defense is a good offense. I took a gamble on myself, and everything worked out. I can always bet on me.

"You must always be prepared to place a bet on yourself, on your future, by heading in a direction that others seem to fear."

~ Robert Green

5

BUILD YOUR CONFIDENCE

"Self-esteem means knowing you are the dream."

~ OPRAH WINFREY

BET ON YOU!

Don't let the past control your future or success. Test your ability and maintain a strong mental capacity. Be clear regarding your vision and accelerate your goals. Surround yourself with like-minded people going where you want to go, doing what you want to do, and having the same dreams and goals.

Every obstacle is an illusion. You will always get what you visualize. The clearer the picture, the more you see, and the quicker your vision becomes a reality. It was time to finish what I had started. So, I set my sights on finishing my degree. I made a long-term decision in an instant. I resigned from my fantastic job at ASCAP to return to my hometown to complete college. Mission accomplished!

Although necessary, it was a bittersweet moment to say farewell to New York, my new friends, my Great Aunt Helen, and a great mentor. I could hear Les Brown in my ear, saying, "Hope in the future gives you power in the present."

I graduated from The Florida A&M University School of Business and Industry with a Bachelor of Science degree in Business Administration with honors.

Upon graduation, I accepted a job in my hometown, making about a quarter of my expected salary. I was upside down on my investment and decided to do something. I started growth opportunities. I wanted more.

While still living in Florida, I applied for a promotional opportunity in Atlanta. I was interviewed on a Saturday and offered the job that same day.

As customary, I waited for the offer letter to arrive in the mail… and nothing. My hopes turned into depression. I wrestled with self-pity.

I could not understand why I never received my offer letter. Finally, my husband said to me, "Let's go get your job." My confidence had plummeted. I was hesitant. The way he spoke to me stirred something within and gave me the confidence to go for it.

Follow through, even when your self-esteem has taken a hard hit and you feel like the odds are against you. Sometimes things do not happen to you, they happen for you.

Had I not made the crucial decision to go for it, I would never have succeeded. My decision to try a second time was gold. I remained with that company for ten years.

I experienced a career differentiator with that company that transformed my thinking and altered my approach to solving problems. I enrolled in a unique leadership development program championed by Jack Welch, the former CEO of General Electric and President of NBC. I attained a

BET ON YOU!

Black Belt in Lean Six Sigma—a powerful team-based approach to improve business processes, increase revenue, decrease waste, and improve customer satisfaction.

I began investing time in listening to Les Brown's speech *"It's Not Over Until You Win,"* and reading dozens of books. I read books by successful people, from Emily Post's *Etiquette, Guide to Modern Manners*, to Napoleon Hill's *Think and Grow Rich*, James Allen's *As a Man Thinketh,* Stephen Covey's books on leadership, and Robert Greene's *The 48 Laws of Power*. Based on the books that I read, I felt ready for the world. I applied their wisdom to my life. I experienced increased confidence, constant improvement in my personal beliefs, and a strong desire to manifest my destiny.

I had graduated against all odds, was experienced at my job, and had a strong work ethic that separated me from the rest. Whenever I tried to move to the next level in my career, I kept bumping my head at the top of the "glass ceiling." I wanted more!

I set my sights on earning an MBA. Remember, I was still running a family, had children in school, and was also a wife. I was juggling all those things while investing in myself because I knew it was the key to my success.

I attempted to get my MBA a few times. I tried first as an

undergraduate in Florida. When I got accepted into Florida A&M, I attended the five-year MBA program at the School of Business and Industry. I dropped out because it was too demanding for me as a non-traditional student, wife, and mother.

Several years later, I tried again while living in Atlanta. I almost completed it on my second attempt through a Georgia State University program for executives. I was six credits short of achieving it... Six!

Then, life happened. My job ended after 10 years. Ironically, I was not upset about the situation, but my colleagues were. I told them to cheer up; when one door closes, another opens. An attitude of gratitude is great gain.

During my tenure at that job, I earned six figures, acquired a Black Belt in Lean Six Sigma, and purchased two beautiful dream homes. My oldest son attended a prominent college in Atlanta, while my younger children attended private schools. In other words, life was good considering from whence we came.

I learned how to lead people and facilitate the transformation and success of others. I was a pragmatic executive who was mentored and coached by some of the best to lead people and encourage others to succeed. Priceless!

BET ON YOU!

Excited about the next chapter of my life, I began sharpening my skills by reading more personal development books to set myself apart. I read books like, *The Greatest Salesman in the World, The Science of Getting Rich, The Richest Man in Babylon, The Art of War, 33 Strategies of War, The Art of Seduction, The Art of Making Money,* and even *The Power of Positive Thinking.* As a result, I gained an elevated mindset about knowing the difference between poverty and wealth. There is no legacy without currency.

Subsequently, I joined various direct sales companies and sold everything from washing powder, toothpaste, girdles, vitamins, juice, coffee, tea—even water!

Build your confidence. Refuse to allow your external environment or situation to dictate your confidence within or your ability to earn money.

"Do not overestimate the competition and underestimate yourself. You are better than you think."
~ T. Harv Eker

6

WHEN THE HORSE DIES, DISMOUNT

"You've got to learn to leave the table when love's no longer being served."

~ NINA SIMONE

BET ON YOU!

Dead horses do not run, and self-sabotaging people do not win. Power is about how to leverage and seize opportunities to your advantage.

When you refuse to confront your situations, you concede. Facing situations requires passion, resourcefulness, persistence, and courage. It is okay to go back to the stable to find your new champion horse and get unstuck.

Why do people refuse to act on things that make them unhappy or are unhealthy? They are afraid of the unknown. When the level of authority exceeds the level of intelligence, there will inevitably be a conflict.

Even when people are in abusive relationships, have terrible jobs, are broke, or clueless about the future, they often remain in lose-lose situations because they are familiar with the pain and problems in that space.

You cannot win any race with a dead horse. If your horse is going nowhere or if the horse you are riding dies, here is a clue: Dismount! It is time to go back to the stable and saddle up a new horse. If you are riding a champion horse, stay on that horse and do not let go.

Are you able to identify the dead horses in your life? Can you identify the stalled horse at the gate when all the other horses gallop down the track? Do you have the courage to get

WHEN THE HORSE DIES, DISMOUNT

off and find a new one?

Dismounting bad horses can be difficult because of feelings of failure, caring about the opinions of others, or trying to avoid a setback. Eagles land to take off.

I left my corporate career and got involved in thriving, direct sales businesses. Soon, I began earning three times the salary I was paid at my job. I also gained valuable tools and success strategies from several champions in the direct sales industry.

I began riding that high horse, making money, and having lots of fun. I had not worked a job for over two years. Eventually, that horse began to unravel. The money started decreasing.

Dismounting is not easy. Sometimes, things are sunk, and you will never recover your invested time, money, or even the value you added if you walk away.

There is a saying that you cannot keep throwing valuable resources after un-fruitful things, hoping they will improve. We must stand bold and cut our losses. I dismounted from the direct sales high horse and went back to my champion horse—corporate America, instead of focusing on a fun horse ride but very volatile.

So, find your vibrant stallion and dis-mount the dead one.

BET ON YOU!

I got back on my champion horse to realize my vision. At the time, I was broke, behind on my rent, had no running water and no electricity.

My youngest son and I shared candles for light as we went from room to room. I even showered, did my hair and make-up at the clubhouse gym in my apartment complex.

What did I do? I created a vision board by candlelight with pictures of things that I wanted to have, be, do, and see in my vision and intention for my life.

I did not allow the darkness to hinder my ability to see a future. Never allow desperation to undermine your ability to negotiate what you want. I had a dream that was bigger than me. It was not about what I was paid to do but what I was *created* to do.

Anchor your belief in something bigger than you. Believe in your talents and invest in yourself to ride the horse of your dreams.

Stop trying to hold on to expired relationships. Let them go; you never needed them anyway. You can never benefit from something that is expired.

We experience setbacks to come back stronger and wiser than before. You can turn your life around. Realize your value and allow yourself to dismount. Overcome your fear and take

WHEN THE HORSE DIES, DISMOUNT

on the world.

> *"The difference between FEELING yourself in action, here and now, and visualizing yourself in action, as though you were on a motion-picture screen, is the difference between success and failure."*
>
> ~ Neville Goddard

7

**START THINKING
ABOUT RESULTS**
BE A STAR

"Always stay true to yourself and never let what somebody else says distract you from your goals"
~ MICHELLE OBAMA

BET ON YOU!

You win some, and you lose some. Results are a consequence, effect, or conclusion of or an outcome of something. Anybody can play a good hand and win. It takes skill, tenacity, and perseverance to take a bad hand, play it, and win.

When you see someone progressing through the ranks, do not hate. You may see their glory, but you do not know their story, or the price paid.

A Langston Hughes' poem entitled, *Mother to Son*, is one of my favorite poems. The poem is a constant reminder that just because *"life ain't been no crystal stair,"* it is not an excuse to turn back, sit down, or fall down the steps. Flip all excuses for failing into reasons to succeed.

Procrastination is suicide on a payment plan. Work on yourself every day to increase your awareness and raise your level of thinking. You become what you think. Getting your mind right establishes the right mindset and framework to enable you to think bigger, better, and faster.

You can be successful despite situations, circumstances, and terrible odds. If you want to improve, you can. Start by setting small goals and celebrating the wins to start the momentum towards achievement. It is like a snowball effect; the results may start small, grow significantly, become more prominent, better, and faster. Keep winning until it becomes a habit.

Rather than exhausting your efforts comparing and competing, duplicate what works, for whom, and under what conditions. Identify your goals and be willing to make the sacrifices.

Put in ten thousand hours of work, pulling the greatness out of yourself. Be willing to take a risk by sharing it with the world.

There are steps you must climb on the ladder to success. No one can climb them for you. These are your decisions and choices to make. If you want to change your behavior to achieve success, you will have to win the battle in your mind first. Then, you must do the work.

My biological father and I eventually reconnected. He was very proud of my accomplishments and told me that I was a rose that grew up in the desert. He said, "You cannot be a star if you do not want to be a star." That spoke volumes to me, and I will never forget it.

Never give up on your dreams and goals. No matter how hard it may get, you are closer than you have ever been.

I was offered a career opportunity at Tennessee State University as the Director of Special Projects and Strategic

Initiatives. I relocated to the Home of the Country Music Hall of Fame, amid a turbulent marriage laden with irreconcilable differences. I welcomed the opportunity and the divine providence that followed. I needed strategies, I needed solutions, and I needed results.

While working full-time, I enrolled in the Executive MBA Program at Tennessee State University. As a result, I experienced another trip of a lifetime—a global immersion in Tokyo, Japan (which was on my vision board) to learn about the culture, hear from renowned CEOs and chairmen, and receive a fantastic opportunity to witness operational excellence in action.

It was time to conquer the MBA. I blasted through the MBA glass ceiling in a one-year accelerated pace at the top of my class. Others in my program were CEOs, dentists, presidents, and other C-level executives, nationally and internationally. The 16-year-old teenage parent and high school dropout had come a long way. Achieving my goals made me understand that it takes follow-through and persistence to reach them. Satisfaction comes when you manifest your dreams and vision.

I had to get out of my way and level up. I had to eliminate the obstacles. I had to bet on myself. I became known for operational excellence as a Lean Six Sigma Black Belt, which sharpened my vision and fueled my desire to become a multimillionaire.

The ultimate currency is you. Start thinking about results, and your mindset will put you in the top 10% of all people. You do not have to be a superstar. When you begin seeing consistent results, your accomplishments will be huge.

Successful people frequently say that failure was a part of their journey. Michael Jordan, one of my favorites, said he lost almost 300 games. Twenty-six times, he was trusted by the team to take the game-winning shot and missed. He said he failed repeatedly. That is why he has succeeded.

There is a valid reason why graduations, championships, and playoffs are valuable. Each of them represents a rite of passage or a sign of accomplishment. They symbolize excellence and the conclusion of a matter. Would you prefer a championship ring or a participation ring?

Everyone likes to win. Winning is good! It builds up self-confidence and boosts self-esteem. It gives us hope that we can become even more significant through the next endeavor.

It is not how you start but how you finish. Think about the results you want to achieve and intentionally eliminate a status quo mindset. Clarity of vision accelerates your results, and you will begin to see your dreams become a reality.

It is impossible to start moving forward without first focusing your mind on the possibilities you see for yourself. External events should never destroy your self-view. With focus and motivation, anything is possible.

"You can't have a million-dollar dream with a minimum wage work ethic."

~ STEPHEN C. HOGAN

8

SET BOUNDARIES

LOVE YOURSELF

"Your time and energy are precious. You get to choose how you use it. You teach people how to treat you by deciding what you will and won't accept."

~ Anna Taylor

BET ON YOU!

*P*rioritization of self is not selfish; it is self-love. Make choices that honor yourself. Life happens to everyone. We will get rejected, lied to, betrayed, abused, cheated, and criticized unfairly by hurtful people. Nevertheless, these external events should never destroy your self-esteem.

Never suffer in silence. If we are quiet about our issues, they will not get resolved, and could lead to larger problems down the road.

As a little girl growing up, my grandmother made sure that I dressed well every day. She would buy me three-piece suits and patent leather, Mary Jane shoes to wear to school. She believed in dressing up daily to reflect class and poise. I felt like a fairytale princess going to a ball because I was always sharp with my suits on.

Every Saturday, she took me to the hair salon to have my hair coiffed in Shirley Temple curls, which I still love to this day. I believed that I was royalty. I knew no other way. Every day, I dressed like it was Easter Sunday! She would always give me money to go to school to buy snacks. I would buy candy instead.

When I was in the third grade, there was a bully at my school that everybody was afraid of because she was huge and had family clout. Every single day, she demanded my candy. I was intimidated. I gave it to her. I thought she picked on me because I dressed nicely. My grandmother just made it look like we had it all together.

I put up with her bullying for most of the year. One day, I reached my limit. I did not care how big she was. I was not even concerned about her gang of cousins. I knew that if she got in a fight, they were going to jump in, too. I no longer cared.

When she demanded my candy that day, I said, "No." All of my classmates were in disbelief that I even attempted to challenge her. I was willing to fight, and it was not going to be over until I won. At that moment, I knew that I was not going to give her my candy anymore. She could not believe it!

We fought—and I lost—but I did gain respect and power that day. She and her family no longer bullied me. I might have lost the fight, but I still won.

Stand up for yourself and seize your power. Know who you are. Do not allow others to intimidate you with anything that makes you feel inferior.

Through therapy, I reclaimed my life from dysfunction, abuse, manipulation, toxic relationships and surviving domestic violence.

Therapy helped me realize I lacked boundaries. Because I

did not have proper boundaries, I allowed people to take advantage of me. I was always Tonya with the "S" on my chess in a fabulous Superwoman cape with a fur collar to match. I was ready to solve everybody's problems but my own.

I was a people pleaser who needed to be delivered. I went along with what others wanted to keep them happy while I suffered in silence. This trait was counterproductive to achieving my goals based on my vision.

One day I told myself, *if you want to change some things, you have to change some things!* It was time to re-evaluate my boundaries and start standing up for myself, whether people liked it or not.

I am still reaping big dividends. Therapy trained me to look inward and realize that the answers to my problems were already within. It helped me realize that I had personal power and how to use it.

There are three critical distinctions in the mind which you use to make better decisions:

1. The first mind is the emotional mind. It tells you what you want to do when you are "in the moment."

SET BOUNDARIES

2. The second mind is the reasonable mind. It is the mind that tells you what you should do. I established boundaries using my reasonable mind. It was crucial to maintaining my well-being. I started by saying the word "no."

3. The third mind is the wise mind. It considers the pros and the cons and helps us make a sound decision between two choices.

Good boundaries require the ability to say "no." Always saying "yes" implies that others are more important than you. You become busier and busier, having little time remaining to enjoy your life. Now, you are frustrated and take it out on everybody else, and people think you are crazy.

I know what it feels like to be trapped in the world of "yes." My grandmother encouraged me to be agreeable and go along to get along.

As I evolved into leadership roles in the corporate world, I realized that I would have to toughen up. Saying "no" is not ugly; it is a way of telling others that you are worth it and that you are an emotionally healthy person with value. There are times when we have to say "no" to good things to have time for great things. You must accept the reality that you cannot please everybody.

BET ON YOU!

Empowering yourself to say "no" means being respectful of your time, energy, and space. I have identified and confronted my issues and the monsters that took advantage of my inability to advocate for myself.

After therapy, I was fully capable of standing my ground. I established healthy boundaries for my life and made them known. I no longer allowed these types of people in my space: Toxic people, negative people, controlling people, manipulators, judgmental people, complacent people, and most importantly, violent people.

Honor yourself to invoke positivity, healing, and prosperity over your life. Therapy helped me emerge as the bold, competent, secure, and assertive woman I am today! With the proper focus and motivation, anything is possible.

Stay focused. Goals are the fuel to get to your destination. I refuel each day with premium **GAS**. Let me explain what that is.

G is for gratitude. Gratitude is attitude. I begin each day by thinking about something to be grateful for, even if money is funny and change is strange.

A is for affirm. Affirm who you are daily. Do not dwell on what you think you cannot do or how you have failed in the past. Focus on what you can do. Use positive talk instead of negative self-talk. Think about it, if your friends and family spoke to you the way you talk to yourself, would you want them around you?

S is for strategies, systems, and support. I rely on strategies that worked previously. I am systematic because I know success is a system that must be employed. All three of these go together; they are intertwined.

That is my view daily. To participate in the promise, you must practice some principles. Decide today what you are going to do for yourself.

What you focus on expands. Much gathers more and less leads to greater loss. Seek out mentors to provide guidance and insight along your journey.

"Never make someone a priority, when all you are to them is an option."

~ MAYA ANGELOU

KNOW YOUR VALUE

DO NOT EXPECT SOMEONE TO CALCULATE IT FOR YOU

"Too many people overvalue what they are not and undervalue what they are."
~ MALCOM S. FORBES

BET ON YOU!

What are your values? Once you identify the values most important to you, they comprise the roadmap for everything you believe, say, and do. It is called your value system.

A value system is a set of variables that determine the sum of your values demonstrated by your choices. This individualistic concept is based on your desires, aspirations, and core beliefs.

Many people do not have a solid value system; they simply live from moment to moment, clueless about who they are, what they are supposed to do, and why... like a piece of paper drifting in the air. Why is this the case? They often set unrealistic goals that are not SMART— Specific, Measurable, Achievable, Realistic, or Timed. Unrealistic goals result in disappointment, failure and push you away from success.

Value systems are as varied as people. They range from good to bad, with everything else in between. Observing both the famous and the infamous, you can see the behavioral outgrowth of their value priorities and get a good idea of who they are. We can see their foundational value cores based on their behavior. What about you? Can you put the finger on your main values in life?

Let's examine the character attributes of a healthy value

KNOW YOUR VALUE

system to use as the basis for your success: The risks you take, the company you keep, and the thoughts you think. Review the following words and prioritize them in the order of importance to you:

Love

Peace

Integrity

Accountability

Responsibility

Happiness

Trust

Truth

Ambition

Success

Goals

Wealth

Fame

Success

Vision

Destiny

Purpose

Health

Spirituality

Social Media Followers

Now, pick the most important word from this list and make that your core value in life. Next, choose five more words that are important to you. These make up the components of your system of values.

As you embrace these essential values, your decision-making skills, goals, behavior, interactions, and communication with others will follow suit. As you evolve and become more conscious, you may adjust your value system and develop new ways of thinking. You will behave in a way that complements your age and maturity level. Your value system will always mirror the real you at the current time in your life.

I know my value system very well. It is my ultimate guide in life. The center of it is the character trait of integrity. Each decision and action must be based on integrity. That is my lead value.

Having integrity means doing the right things right. Taking a shortcut might get you lost or prolong the journey. It is not what you do; it is *how* you do it. How you do anything is how you do everything.

I value a commitment to excellence, personal accountability, responsibility, and empathy. Sometimes, having empathy gets me into trouble, bordering on enabling, however, integrity helps me differentiate between enabling and empathy.

Know your values and live by them. Be humble and remain poised. Money and success only magnify who you are. Do not let fame and success go to your head. Be genuinely you. Maintaining a healthy value system is something you will never have to apologize for or regret later.

In addition to having a healthy value system, these are some steps to achieving a healthy balance financially, mentally, and emotionally:

1. Singleness of Purpose

Consistency, follow-through, and having a singleness of purpose are the difference between success and failure. Consistency demands two hard decisions: how to start and how to finish.

Follow One Course Until Successful (FOCUS). We must finalize what we start if we ever want to realize the joy of achievement.

I have always had one more idea to try, one more conclusion before stopping, and always coming up with new ways to make something better. I had to discipline myself to quiet my innovative mind and focus on completing something successfully.

Instead of having a litany of unfinished projects, done is better than perfect. That piece of advice has helped me to stay focused and complete what I have started before starting something new.

Maximize your focus and minimize any distractions. There is no point in looking at other people and measuring your life using their standards. That is unproductive time and energy. You are not them, and they are not you. Start building your success using successful strategies.

2. Follow-Through

Follow-through requires you to have discipline, courage, and conviction. There are no results without follow-through. Look at the strategic steps successful people use.

I continue to implement and evaluate these strategies to ensure I am on track, in the right place at the right time, and with the right people. Keep your eye on the prize.

3. Eliminate Success Crushers

Make a list of all the people and things in your life that

are not worthy of you and eliminate them. You cannot force a person to have good taste; if they do not want to embrace your dreams or aspirations, let them go.

Whenever you associate with unsuccessful people or engage in unproductive behavior, you limit your potential. Failure, lack of success, and an impoverished mindset are contagious! Success crushers include past relationships, experiences that ended badly, memories from the past, bad habits, entanglements, and even addictive behaviors. Eliminate people who do not add value to your life. Your success depends on it.

4. Change Your Friends and Change Your Life

Surround yourself with positive, secure, and inspiring people. Maya Angelou said, "When people show you who they are, believe them." Stop trying to change them into who you want them to be.

Nothing kills a relationship faster than a fake, jealous, selfish, insecure, petty, or disloyal friend. These are often called "frenemies." We have all had them. The only solution to this is to get those squares out of your circle. Let them go. Otherwise, you will become who you do not want to be.

BET ON YOU!

You are only as great as your circle. Do not hold yourself hostage to who you used to be or what is behind you. The key to changing your life is to invest your valuable time with like-minded people.

Most people's value systems differ—y is a function of x. The outcome (y) is a result of inputs (x). Once you determine the values that shape your life, you will have clarity of who you are and what is important to you.

Always stay true to your system. Follow the advice of Polonius in Shakespeare, *"Above all, to thine own self, be true."* You can think your way to success. Remember, it is all a matter of perception.

"Thoughts become things. If you see it in your mind, you will hold it in your hand."

~ BOB PROCTOR

10

YOUR FRIENDS BECOME YOU

(AND VICE VERSA)

"The friend must be like money, that before you need it, the value is known."

~ SOCRATES

BET ON YOU!

Form the habit of applying and using positive emotions to effect the change you seek. Several variables in life determine success or failure. The one constant that is a critical force in determining your professional and personal life is friends.

Friends come in all sizes, shapes, colors, behaviors, and backgrounds. They also etch their opinions on your soul; their influence in your life is undeniable, for better or for worse.

A significant starting point for success is evaluating and eliminating the types of "friends" in your life who do not add value. Make some tough decisions. Sometimes you will have to let go of people who cannot go to the next phase of your life with you. The further you go, the lighter the cargo.

Do not let people sit around your fire unless they are adding logs to keep the flames burning. If they do not add logs to your fire, they steal the heat or douse water on your flame. They do not want you to become a butterfly; instead, they want you to remain a caterpillar forever.

The difference between medicine and poison is in the dosage. The Creator is greater than the creation, and the thinker is greater than the thought. Your concept of self will determine your future.

Eagles do not fly with chickens, and chickens do not have

wings to fly, only to fry. People are either attached to you or assigned to you—know the difference. If they are not authorized to be with you, they tamper with your destiny.

Let's consider the qualities you should look for in a friend. The first quality is **honesty**. Finding an honest friend is like finding a needle in a haystack. You need genuine friends to make your life work.

They are either daily infusions of positivity or negativity. A friend can make or break you, depending on their way of thinking. If you invest your time with friends who tell the truth and have a high moral character, the odds are that you will too. That's a good thing.

When I lived in New York, I met some wonderful friends. I also met a friend who was not so wonderful. She was a functional drug addict with a terrific job at an investment firm. She had a beautiful son she adored. During one of our girls' nights out, her addiction revealed itself. I saw my friend using drugs. I could not believe my eyes. She even offered to share them with me. I declined the invitation by politely saying "no" and "thank you." I was very concerned and determined that she and I would have a crucial conversation.

The perfect opportunity arose to address the situation. As fate would have it, we ended up stuck on the train together in the subway station. At that time, I expressed how detrimental her behavior was to our continued friendship and her overall quality of life. She thanked me for expressing concern. We eventually parted ways and lost contact with each other.

Honest friends are willing to have crucial conversations about preserving the integrity and quality of the friendship. Stop blaming others for your behavior! Own your truth.

The second quality is **dependability**. A real friend is dependable; fake friends abandon you in times of need. Real friends add value to you when you are falling apart, supporting you in every way, even in times when you are not there for yourself. This type of confidant is price-less.

When you find yourself in a bind, an embarrassing scenario, a downward spiral, a funk, or even a seemingly impossible situation, those are the times when real friends are there to provide support in a variety of ways. They may take you out for a drink, listen to you vent, get you out of the house, do something fun, provide money to help you through a financial problem, or simply remind you that everything is going to be okay.

The third quality is **trustworthiness**. Real friends do what they say, keep their promises, show up on time, give you great advice, and can always be counted on to come through.

YOUR FRIENDS BECOME YOU

When it comes to a friend, you need faithfulness and not fakeness. Choose wisely.

The fourth quality is **loyalty**. It is the essence of any friendship. Any friend who gossips about you, misrepresents you around others, or betrays you is not a friend. When you find loyal friends, they are worth their weight in gold.

The fifth quality is **ambition**. If you surround yourself with friends who have lofty ambitions and significant drive, they are contagious and will inspire you. Your standard of success will begin to match theirs. The more winners you have in your circle, the more likely you are to become a winner. The same is true for losers.

If friends want the absolute best for themselves, they will always want the best for you. Bond and connect with them. Enjoy the company of people who sincerely compliment you, encourage you, believe in you, support you, and always want the best for you. Follow them to the top!

Friends are vital to your success and can be just as detrimental to your failure. Be selective. You only get one grand recital at life, so make sure to invite the right people.

*"You are the average of
the five people you spend the most time with. Choose wisely."*

~ JIM ROHN

11

BE EXTRAORDINARY

"If you are always trying to be normal you will never know how amazing you can be."

~ Maya Angelou

BET ON YOU!

You cannot make thousandnaire moves and expect millionaire results. If you genuinely want to become great, start thinking, acting, and behaving with a millionaire mindset. Millionaires play to win.

Here is a piece of advice about winning in Las Vegas: If you want to go home with a thousand dollars, do not bring a hundred dollars to gamble. The reality of Vegas is that you must bring a thousand to win a hundred. Life is like that, too! The higher the stakes, the higher the potential return on investment (ROI).

To be successful, you must stand out and be distinct. Extraordinary must become the norm for you, not the exception. The average of anything is normal. Separate yourself; be extraordinary. Some are can-do people, and others are can't-do people.

If you are always doing what others are doing, you will consistently have ordinary results. You will reach a point in your life when you are forced to leave the safety of your comfort zone or become sick and tired of living on a basic level. Either way, it is time to change frequencies.

Change can be difficult, but comfort stunts growth. You can be the most amazing jump roper in the world. Try Double Dutch—same ropes, different skills. There are levels to success

BE EXTRAORDINARY

Some ropes you can skip and some ropes you need to know.

To change the game, you must be a game-changer. You either see the glass half full or half empty. It is all a matter of perspective and how you see through your eyes. If you see yourself as average, you accept your fate. If you want to be looked at differently, people must see you differently.

Let the world know that you exist! It can be tempting to adjust your shine to make others comfortable. Blowing out someone else's candle will not make yours shine brighter.

Do not let anyone dim your light. Come out of hiding. Be brave. Stand in your spotlight. The disease to please is the enemy. Be you—bold, assertive, confident, and honest. Tell yourself it is time to level up and achieve your goals and dreams.

Be unique and extraordinary. Take inventory of everything in your life: your clothes, hobbies, habits, conversations, lifestyle, and the way you come across to others. Make some fundamental changes to shift your mindset and shatter any limiting beliefs that hold you back.

Start taking strategic risks and be intentional about what you want. The new you will succeed as a result. This often comes after putting in 10,000 hours to sharpen your craft and achieve greatness. Commit to constant progression.

The most crucial trait that contributes to success is a strong focus. If you believe in the power of focus, you will achieve extraordinary results. Focus on what you want and seize it.

How focused are you? Are you able to decide on one goal, stick with it and build all your decisions around it until you succeed? If you struggle with focus, there are mentors, teachers, and coaches that can help. Lean on them and listen to their advice. Let them provoke your thinking pattern. Iron always sharpens iron; that is called a support system. It is an essential ingredient to success.

Until you take the first step, none of the others can follow. When you feel the impetus to move, do so. When you start moving, nothing can stop you. Your new journey has begun. If you contemplate, overthink, or procrastinate, the window of opportunity will pass.

Where you are going is more important than where you have been. Everyone can make a wrong decision the first time. That is called a lesson learned. If we do not learn and continue to do the same thing, that is called foolishness. Do not be a fool.

Never relent. Step out and step up. Allow the world to see

what you possess. Acknowledge what you have to offer to the world.

Do not go with the crowd, illuminate. Promote yourself and enjoy the attention. Attention attracts money. Stop working for money and make money work for you.

Think big. You control your destiny. Understand how to use your mind's wisdom and the power of your will to direct your behavior towards the destination of your desired success.

"Successful people do things that the average person is not willing to do. They make sacrifices the average person is not willing to make. But the difference it makes is extraordinary."

~ BRIAN TRACY

12

ELEVATE YOUR CHARACTER

"Don't let someone who gave up on their dreams talk you out of yours."

~ Zig Ziglar

BET ON YOU!

What is Character? Character is a trait that is developed—good or bad. Character is not who you are when everyone is watching, but who you are when no one is watching. Character is not what you say but what you do. Character is a trait that cannot be faked! It is your DNA.

Let me provide you with some successful strategies to become a valuable, betting commodity, achieve your goals, and bet on you to win.

1. **Be patient.** As you begin, you will encounter failures, perhaps several of them. Do not panic. Life is a marathon, not a sprint. Stay the course and flip failures into successes. Keep a long-term mindset. You will get there.

2. **Take massive action.** The best way to take advantage of a low point in your life is to take massive action. Whether you fail or succeed, keep reminding yourself, *Win, lose or draw, I am always betting on me. I am the most valuable commodity* (MVC)!

3. **Stay focused.** If you stray away from your foundation, goals, and dreams, you will lose your way. Refuse to let circumstances, relationships, or unexpected events distract you from your focus. Distractions are constant, like change; it is up to you whether you will become distracted.

ELEVATE YOUR CHARACTER

Turn adversity into an opportunity and make the best of every situation. Instincts are crucial to your success. Respond to the unexpected like a winner. Anyone can do well when everything is already great. You are your life. Success is customary for you. Focus on the future you want to create and think of the actions you need to manifest.

4. **Set goals.** Set a goal and achieve it with tenacity, discipline, and follow-through. The great oil billionaire, H. L. Hunt, said that there are only two fundamental requirements for success: first, decide what you want; second, determine the price you will pay. This is what separates the good from the great.

5. **Be consistent.** Ten thousand (10,000) hours of consistent practice is the key to success (The Outliers, Malcolm Gladwell). The way to become excellent at anything requires constant effort. Success is not a secret; it is a system. You must make yourself do what you should do when you should do it, whether you feel like it or not. You must put in the work.

6. **Take responsibility.** Nothing ever happens to us by chance. It does not matter if your life is or has been filled with poverty, violence, alcoholism, drug addiction, sexual abuse, or family illiteracy, you do not have to accept that as your fate.

BET ON YOU!

Act like where you are going, not where you have been. Stated another way: Dress for the job you want, not the job you have. Take responsibility for your life and decide to shift things around to make a difference. The choices we make today shape our future.

7. **Do not quit.** The world did not end when I lost everything and filed for bankruptcy. I kept trying until I found a way to win. Thomas Edison tried over 10,000 times to make a light bulb before he succeeded. Even if you have been dealt a bad hand, remain intentional, resilient, and willing to persevere to accomplish your end-game goals and dreams.

8. **Take risks.** Every successful man or woman is a risk-taker. Do not get too secure and stable that you resist change, avoid taking risks or dread making big decisions. There must be a burning desire to grow and trade up for something bigger and better. Have a "why" that scares you or makes you cry. The difference between success and failure is that failure runs away from fears while success runs towards them. Timing is everything. The best time to innovate and take risks is when you are struggling. Be persistent and patient. Stay the course.

9. **Find your tribe.** Behind every successful person is another person. You need people who are on or above your

level to help you achieve your dreams and not compete with them. You are only as great as your circle. When you find other people that identify and relate to you, do not outgrow them, take them with you. You cannot do it alone. It takes a team to win a championship. You need experienced mentors, coaches, and partners.

10. **Create value.** Value attracts wealth and attention. Success is solving a problem. Find a problem that your knowledge, skills, passions, dreams, and potential are designed to solve. Someone needs what you have to offer. You were created to solve a specific problem. Address that problem, and success is inevitable.

These principles will pay significant dividends in your self-investing life as you decide to make them habits.

"Never measure your progress using someone else's ruler."
~ ANONYMOUS

13

SET MEASURABLE GOALS

"If you set goals and go after them with all the determination you can muster, your gifts will take you places that will amaze you."

~ LES BROWN

BET ON YOU!

How do you handle goals and dreams? Do you enjoy setting them, adjusting them, following them, and completing them?

When you want to succeed, goals and dreams must be created and sustained. In the careers of most successful people, goals and dreams are invaluable.

Let me share a proven system with you to become more goal-oriented:

1. List your priorities and begin with a big **why**. Make a general list of your career values and place them in a set of future goals. These may include categories like your net worth, finances, income, family, career, salary, clients, health and fitness, travel, vacations, future projections, property, and asset management.

2. Place your priority list in order of importance. Do this with a lot of thought and evaluation.

3. Add goals under each of your general categories. For example, under net worth, you will set specific goals. List the overall category and then clearly define the goals under it. Make the goal tailor-made for you.

SET MEASURABLE GOALS

List three types of goals: **Long-term** -10 years from now; **Medium-term** -5 years from now; and **Short-term** - 1 year from now.

1) What would you like to be doing?
2) How much money do you want to make?
3) What kind of relationship do you want?
4) What type of home do you want?
5) What kind of car do you want to drive?
6) Where would you like to travel?

Then, list your daily, weekly, and monthly priorities. Make a general list of all the things you want to accomplish in the next thirty (30) days.

Separate your goals into daily, weekly, and monthly segments. These "small" steps will help you manage your short-term goals.

Organize your daily priorities in order of importance that day by asking, *What are the top three things I want to accomplish today?*

BET ON YOU!

1. _____
2. _____
3. _____

Schedule a one-hour meeting with yourself to reflect and review your goal progress. Complete the most manageable tasks first. When you accomplish your first goal, highlight it in green and move on to your second goal.

One by one, complete your daily priority list. As you approach each new goal, ask yourself, *Is this necessary or unnecessary?* If unnecessary, cross it off the list and move on to the next item.

Adjust your daily list if it needs any tweaking. Do not fall into the trap of "Superhero," where you believe you must save the world. When you try to save others, be careful you don't drown in the process.

It is prudent to put your mask on first before trying to save someone else. You will soon figure out what you can and cannot realistically accomplish.

If your strategy is right, you can win the game of life with nothing. Posture your life using my Ace High Model to Always Commit to Excellence (ACE) by knowing where to play, what to do, and how to win.

SET MEASURABLE GOALS

ACE HIGH MODEL

"A dream written down with a date becomes a goal. A goal broken down into steps becomes a plan. A plan backed by action makes your dreams come true."

~ GREG S. REID

14

BET ON YOU!

"You miss 100% of the shots you don't take."

~ Wayne Gretzky

BET ON YOU!

Bet on **you** to win! The best risk you could ever take is to bet on you. Bet big. It is a win-win and not either/or.

You can have this **and** that. You can have what you say and what you want. What if I gave up when people talked about me being a teenage mother and a high school dropout? What if I let go after people told me my dreams of obtaining higher education were not possible when I was 25 years old with three kids? What if I trusted every naysayer who tried to minimize and marginalize me to their limiting beliefs? What if I believed them?

I decided that the odds would work in my favor, and I won. Your dream is not for everybody. Terminate dream killers.

Never let someone convince you that you cannot do something. Protect your dream. People will project their fears on you because they refuse to take chances. Ignore the naysayers, move in silence, and be strategic. Sometimes it is necessary to make a clean break to start over and build yourself up again on new ground. The element of surprise is powerful.

Belief is the foundation of everything great. If you want something, get it. Believe you are exceptional before anyone else does.

BET ON YOU!

Think about this: Because you exist, you have already won. You triumphed in the first race of your life! Everything that occurs in your life after that is for your greatest good.

How we spend our time shows what we value. Self-investment is like investing in stocks, bonds, annuities, money markets, and real estate. You are your most valuable commodity (MVC). You possess the power, knowledge, skills, and ability to manifest the life of your dreams.

How we spend our time shows what we value. Be selective about where you invest your time, money, and resources. Do not spread yourself too thin; optimize your time and resources by leveraging your distinctive competencies.

A detour is not a dead end. It is just a reroute. Sometimes you might have to take the stairs instead of having the luxury of an elevator to ease the climb. This process can even be painful. Be patient and persistent.

Madam C. J. Walker became the first black female millionaire in America during a recession. She was an entrepreneur with goals and dreams, who came out of the cotton fields, who promoted herself by manufacturing hair care products, and who built her factory
according to her dream.

BET ON YOU!

You can create more excellent outcomes than you currently have by believing in yourself. Decide to succeed today, and nothing can stop you. Do not let anyone turn your sky into a ceiling.

Decide who you want to be and find your purpose. Set your intention on it and follow that blueprint for success.

Money is made when you operate on purpose. Mansa Musa, the King of Mali, was the richest man ever, with a $400 billion net worth. He was the embodiment of success and winning. Follow his lead.

Gaining money is an action. Maintaining money is a behavior. Multiplying money is knowledge. Spend time with people who show you how to grow money.

Embrace your resources and leverage them to advance your purpose. Success comes with stipulations. Be agile enough to change and adapt to those requirements to sustain your success.

Be self-aware. No one knows you or your business better than you. Establish your persona, develop your style, and then dominate it. It is like a magical winning streak. You are hot, one success after another, win after win after win. That is what positions you to launch yourself to greatness.

BET ON YOU!

Know your distinctive competencies. This is your "it factor" that makes you great. Push forward, be driven, and do not panic. This is a lifetime commitment.

Remember, the equation y is a function of x. What you get out of anything is a function of what you put into it. Lean Six Sigma your life with precision and accuracy. Do the right things right. Be efficient with your time, money, and energy.

Maximize your income, revenue, and profits by doing productive things that yield results. Minimize waste by eliminating unproductive things you know will hinder or distract you. Then, streamline whatever is consuming your time and adds no value. Unleash your greatness—no more excuses. Stop procrastinating and speak it into existence. Decide what YOU want and do it. Opportunity is a window that opens and closes.

The turning point in my life came at the height of my most challenging struggle when I relocated to New York City. Looking back on it today, I cannot believe I dared to do it. The Best defense is a good offense, that is what I did.

Do it now! Launch yourself into greatness and be extraordinary. You can only achieve your potential and realize your purpose when you *Bet on You.*

"Success is not a secret; it is a system."

~ Florence Scovel Shinn

CONCLUSION

"Everything comes at a cost. Just what are you willing to pay for it."

~ Serena Williams

BET ON YOU!

My passion and purpose are to empower, elevate, and equip others to be official, not just beneficial. Invest in relationships with people who inspire and elevate you to achieve massive levels of success. Success is measured by how many people are successful with you.

I have given you the powerful secrets of my success on these pages, as I chose to bet on myself in life, despite the odds. Do not just read them or even believe in them, ACT! It all starts with one great choice to transform your life.

Life is short. Make sure that you are not merely existing in or living in desperation. The world not only needs you; YOU need you.

Keep a long-term mindset. Stay focused. Do not allow circumstances, relationships, or unexpected events to distract you. Quiet any outside noise. Create a strategic plan for your life with a timetable for achievement. Finally, never get emotional about wins or losses. Thus, you cannot get emotional over your successes or failures.

Build up your assets and strengthen your character to make yourself a valuable betting commodity. Your character and strength are your brands. Create social proof, become accomplished, and develop integrity and credibility. Learn from successful pacesetters who are already doing what you

CONCLUSION

want to do.

It is not lonely at the top; it is lonely getting there. The journey is challenging but rewarding, nonetheless.

Many people fall short of applying truths to their lives and die an unfulfilled, unrealized existence full of regret. You do not have to be one of them. There are no limits except the limits you entertain in your mind. The size of your belief determines the size of your success. **Bet on you!**

"You don't make progress by standing on the sidelines, whimpering and complaining. You make progress by implementing ideas."

~ Shirley Chisholm

ABOUT THE AUTHOR

TONYA KILPATRICK, MBA

Founder of Tonya Kilpatrick Global • Executive Coach • Transformational Strategist • Lean Six Sigma Black Belt • Speaker • Author •

"BET ON YOU! ONE MORE TIME"

Tonya Kilpatrick, MBA is the founder of Tonya Kilpatrick Global and The BOSS Life Academy. She is a Transformational Strategist, Speaker, Author, Executive Coach, and Certified Lean Six Sigma Black Belt who uses her more than 25 years of experience in business to inspire, empower and encourage individuals to bet on themselves and shatter unsurmountable odds.

Tonya has motivated, inspired, and led organizations, individuals, teams and executives through successful growth, development, business start-up, strategic planning, and strategy and execution. She is a highly sought-after speaker who advocates for increased productivity and operational excellence in life and business. She also holds certifications in Executive Leadership, Business Process Improvement and Project Management. In addition, she directed an initiative to create a 90-acre Research and Innovation mixed-use district at Tennessee State University to spur economic and community development.

Tonya's motto is *"Excellence is the norm, not the exception."* She has managed over $250 million in grants, built teams and re-engineered processes that have led to increased revenue. Her approach to leadership development, strategy and execution is methodical and systematic to achieve strategic success.

She provides a practical and systematic approach to personal and professional development. Tonya focuses on people, performance and operational excellence and provides the following services:

- Lean Six Sigma Consulting
- Keynote Speaker
- Workshop Presenter
- Online Courses and Training
- Strategy and Execution
- Project Management
- Strategic Planning
- Executive Coaching
- Personal and Leadership Development
- Bet on You Podcast
- Millionaire Mastermind Inner Circle
- Business and Management Consulting

Tonya has the education, experience, and resources to provide strategic solutions that can help you achieve results!

STRATEGIES | SOLUTIONS | RESULTS

"Extraordinary Plans Achieve

Extraordinary Results"

~ TONYA KILPATRICK

**TO BOOK TONYA FOR YOUR NEXT EVENT
CONNECT WITH US AT
WWW.TONYAKILPATRICK.COM**

To start your personal development journey visit

www.thebosslifeacademy. It's time to Bet on You!

RAVE REVIEWS FOR TONYA

"After an impromptu session with Coach TK, I was recharged, and my faith was enlarged. I made the decision to bet on me. Thanks Coach!"

~ *Sakeia M.*

"Tonya's presentation **exceeded our expectations**! She engaged and empowered our team to seize opportunities."

~ *Kiana K., CEO at Korean Polish*

"Ms. Kilpatrick is amazing! She delivered a great talk '**Where to Play, What to Do, and How to Win**' and provided us with tools to implement her strategies."

~ *Gayle B., Executive Director*

www.ingramcontent.com/pod-product-compliance
Lightning Source LLC
Chambersburg PA
CBHW031602110426
42742CB00036B/667